Praise for *"Hope and Healing During the Holidays"*

Grief is often misunderstood. Grief is a natural and necessary process when we experience loss of any kind, whether it is someone close, your health or your job. Jayne's book is focused on the personal loss of family loved ones and the emotional responses of the family members. It also offers much hope and simple solutions through telling her own journey of grief. This book will be of much benefit to many who read her story.
Geraldine Gallagher - Kinesiologist and Neuro Trainer

Hope and Healing During the Holidays After the Loss of a Loved One by Jayne Flaagan is a timely MUST-READ message for those dealing with grief, be it recent or not. Holidays are especially difficult for those who have lost loved ones. Flaagan transparently relates her struggles with her own multiple losses and coping strategies used to combat the loneliness and depression. I would recommend this book, not only for those who have suffered loss, but also for others looking to help another who has.
Majetta Morris, Freelance Editor/Writer

A needed message just in time for the Holidays. Psychologists have known for years that the Holidays can be particularly stressful for those who have lost loved ones during the year, sometimes accompanied by such depression that there seems to be no joy left in the world or the grieving person. Ms. Flaagan used her own experience to handle this difficult time of the year with practical advice. Her easy-to-read book, short enough to be read in an hour, should by read by everyone who has lost someone this past year…and everyone who knows someone who has lost someone.
Mike Lewis

Hope and Healing During the Holidays After the Loss of a Loved One

Jayne Flaagan
Husky Publishing
East Grand Forks, MN U.S.A.
email@djflaagan@gra.midco.net

This book is dedicated to:

***My mother and father (Alva and Willard),
my sister Barbara,
and my brothers Bruce and Greg.***

Copyright © 2014 Jayne Flaagan
Cover Design © 2014 Jayne Flaagan
(angel picture by Michal Osmenda)

All rights reserved. No part of this publication may be reproduced or transmitted in any form or by any means, including informational storage and retrieval systems, without permission in writing from the copyright holder, except for brief quotations in a review.

About the Author

Jayne Flaagan grew up in North Dakota and made the big move to Minnesota many years ago. She lives with her husband and dog named Ella. She also has three great children.

Flaagan writes a series of children's picture books about Ella, appropriately called "**Ella the Doggy**" book series.

Jayne's education and experience includes many years in both Elementary and Early Childhood education. She has degrees in Advertising/Public Relations and French, although she speaks Spanish better than French!

The author loves to travel, read, do crossword puzzles, take walks and spend time with her family, as well as having various other hobbies and past times. Jayne also ran her own Home Childcare Center for over 10 years, as well as a Parent and Child Center for several years.

Forward

Hello. Because you are reading this book, I am guessing that you have lost someone you love. Or, perhaps you know someone else who is grieving the loss of someone.

I have a confession to make: I not only wrote this book for you, but I wrote it for myself, as well. Since last Christmas, I have lost three family members. Before I wrote this book, I found myself asking the same questions that I included in this book. I personally found some answers to many of those questions and I believe that you will too.

When you lose someone you care about, there will always be a part of you that misses that person. During the holidays, you may feel your loved one's absence more than you do at other times of the year. Keep your mind open to the possibilities as you read this book. You will discover many ways that you can help yourself with the grieving process. Some suggestions may help you immediately and some will help you both now and many years down the road.

For the most part, I wrote this book for someone who has lost a loved one due to death. However, I need to acknowledge your loss if you are apart from someone whom you loved or cared about, whatever that reason may be. You may have been in a long-term relationship with someone and no longer are. Perhaps you are separated or divorced. Maybe your spouse is in the military and is deployed this holiday season. When you are grieving the loss of someone, it does not matter why that person is no longer with you. All that matters is that you too have healing to do. I am confident that you will find help in this book.

The information in this book is based on many different perspectives. I have included the advice of experts who deal with grieving individuals on a regular basis, numerous articles that I have read, and the personal experience of both myself and others. These perspectives are from people who have all lost a loved one. We can assure you that between time and being proactive, you will get through the tough times. You may have some bumps along the away, but your days **will** get better and brighter.

If you would like to leave me a personal comment, visit www.livingwithoutsomeoneyoulove.com and write to me. I would love to hear from you.

All my best, Jayne

CHAPTER 1	11
What Will The Holidays Bring?	11
Chapter 2	15
Stages of Grief	15
Chapter 3	22
The Loss of a Child	22
Chapter 4	25
Plan For and Accept Changes	25
Chapter 5	28
Accept Your Feelings	28
Chapter 6	35
Look to God	35
Chapter 7	36
Take Care of Yourself Physically and Emotionally	36
Chapter 8	43
Make Time for Yourself	43
Chapter 9	45
Ask for Support and Help	45
Chapter 10	48
Be Realistic With Expectations of Yourself	48
Chapter 11	53

Talk about Your Loved One 53

Chapter 12 55

Honor Your Loved One 55

Chapter 13 57

Blend Old and New Traditions 57

Chapter 14 61

Focus on the Children 61

Chapter 15 67

Be Thankful 67

Chapter 16 70

Do Something for Someone Else 70

Chapter 17 73

Look Forward with a Positive Attitude 73

Chapter 18 76

If you know someone who is grieving 76

Chapter 19 80

More Resources and Support 80

Chapter 20 85

All we can do is our best 85

CHAPTER 1
WHAT WILL THE HOLIDAYS BRING?

You may be reading this book for the same reason I wrote it. We are looking for answers. We have lost someone we love, either this year – or maybe even several years ago – and we are looking for answers and ways to not only "get through" the holidays, but possibly even enjoy some aspects of the upcoming season.

The holidays, which are supposed to be a time of happiness and feeling good, can be stressful and tiring under normal circumstances. If you are still reeling from the loss of an important person in your life, extra emotions the holidays bring can make us feel very overwhelmed this time of year.

Celebrating may be the furthest thing from your mind right now. You may wonder, as I am, if you'll ever enjoy these special times of the year like you used to.

What can make it even harder is that memories of happy times during past holiday seasons remind us even more of who and what we have lost. These memories remind us how much our life has changed since Christmases past.

The "holidays" can include everything from Halloween and Thanksgiving to Christmas, Chanukah, Ramadan, Kwanza and New Year celebrations. That's a big chunk of time - especially if you are not looking forward to them.

This year may be your first batch of holidays without your loved one. Maybe it's your second or third, or even longer. It doesn't really matter how long ago your loved one passed away if you are still grieving them. We may feel we are well on the road to recovery, yet the emotions and expectations of every holiday season can cause raw emotions to come crashing down on us again.

Some of our fear for the upcoming holidays may be due to the uncertainty of everything. How will I handle these days? Will people understand if I show expressions of grief around them? Am I going to have any energy and motivation to do the things I normally do this time of year – and do I even want to do the same things this year?

For me personally, I will be spending the Holidays with three fewer family members than I did just one year ago.

In April, my mother-in-law unexpectedly passed away. A few weeks later, my father-in-law committed suicide and a few weeks after that, my little brother Greg died in an ATV accident.

You and I may be "in the same boat." If you have lost a loved one as I have, you be wondering what this holiday season will bring. Even though we both may be dealing with similar situations, I do not know your personal story. Nor do I know exactly how you feel or what you are specifically going through as a unique individual.

Neither you nor I will be the first, nor will we be the last, to lose loved ones. That fact does not make our pain any easier. However, knowing so many others have weathered the storm that we are now passing through to once again feel hope and be happy, we too, can expect that for ourselves.

This is not to say we will not always feel some sense of loss, because we probably will. However, with the right attitude, spirit and determination, we can help ourselves through the grieving process.

I don't want to dread the holidays this year - or any other year. I am guessing that you feel the same way or you would not be reading this book.

We owe it to ourselves and those around us, to try and be proactive in our healing. I have experienced many holiday seasons after losing both of my parents, a sister and two brothers. I have learned there are things we can do to help move the healing process along. Some aspects of this holiday season may be hard for us. However, I think both you and I can find moments of joy and gratitude.

Thank you for taking this journey with me.

Chapter 2
Stages of Grief

You have probably heard about the "stages of grief." These stages can be used as general guidelines for how we progress through the grieving process. Since we are all unique individuals, the stages of grief we go through, as well as how we progress through these stages, are going to vary with each person.

We are not all going to follow the same order or the same timeline with each stage. We may skip certain stages. We may regress backwards into a stage every now and then. It might feel like "two steps forward and three steps back," especially during the holidays. We may experience several stages at once or bounce back and forth between stages. We may even get "stuck" in a stage.

It's important to have some background on the typical stages of grief. It can help us prepare for, cope with, and understand some of the feelings we may be experiencing. The stages of grief can also help you determine whether or not you should seek professional help.

Keeping in mind that these are general guidelines, the following are the different stages of grief:

Shock and **Denial**

These two stages may be among the first stages of grief you experience after someone's death. Shock and denial may help absorb some of the loss for us, until bit by bit, we prepare ourselves to accept the finality of what has happened. For obvious reasons, we cannot stay in these stages for a prolonged period of time.

Isolation

This is a very typical stage that may set in after shock and denial wear off. While we do need time alone to process the changes in our life due to a death, it is not a good thing if we find ourselves staying isolated for an extended period of time.

Pain and **Guilt**

These stages often follow the isolation stage. Of all the stages, pain is probably the stage that stays with us the longest.

Whether deserved or not, I cannot think of one person I know who has not felt some degree of guilt after losing someone.

One universal reason for guilt seems to involve not having spent enough time with that person.

As I was writing this chapter, my husband told me he needed to go out of town for a couple of days and invited me to go with him. My first instinct was to tell him that I couldn't go with him because I had too much to do. Immediately afterwards, I started thinking how I would feel if something happened to him on this trip and I had not gone with him. I made the decision to go with him and am so glad I did.

You should not feel badly if someone you love dies and you did not take every opportunity to be with them. In the future, whenever you are able to, take time for your loved ones and appreciate them while they are here. I myself have not perfected this ideal by any means, but I am trying to do better than I have in the past.

Anger and Bargaining

After we begin to accept and deal with our loss, the stages of **anger** and **bargaining** may set in. I really don't recall doing any bargaining after losing someone, but I know I have definitely felt my share of anger, both at the situation itself and towards the person who died.

My Mother-in-Law was such a wonderful and caring person. Before her death, I could never have comprehended being angry with her. Yet, after her death, I felt anger towards her for the first time. I felt that she had let us down when we all still needed her so much.

When my father-in law killed himself, at first I thought that I completely understood. However, after some time had passed, the anger began to creep in, because he obviously could have prevented his death. (Rationally, I do understand the depression that motivated him, but that is a subject in itself that I will not delve into in this book). When my brother Greg died, I was mad at him right away for making the careless decision that caused his life to end. Greg was killed when he attempted to jump over a large rock pile while he was on his ATV.

The anger that I felt about the deaths of both my sister, Barbara and my brother, Bruce actually came before they had passed away.

Barbara had not sought medical treatment for her breast cancer. She was a nurse and "should have known better." Bruce died of melanoma, a skin cancer. My anger with that stemmed from the fact that he often went shirt-less in the summer time and burnt his skin quite frequently. By the time Barbara and Bruce died, anger was no longer an issue.

For each of these deaths, I felt anger at different *stages*, I felt different *degrees* of anger and I felt angry for *varying amounts* of time.

After my Mom and Dad passed away, I honestly don't remember feeling angry. However, years later, we often remember things differently.

Depression and **Loneliness**

These two stages often follow pain and guilt and they may coincide with each other. Not only do they often coincide, but feeling lonely can cause depression, and vice versa. However, because you can be depressed without feeling lonely and you can feel lonely without being depressed, they really are two separate feelings.

Acceptance

Acceptance is usually the final stage of grief. Up to this point and maybe for years to come, you are trying to figure out how to re-build your life without your loved one. You should be feeling better both physically and emotionally by now. As you feel better, you will dread the future less and find things to look forward to. When you think about your loved one, it will be with less pain and more joy. The fact that you have accepted your loss does not mean that you will not grieve any more, but it does mean that at least you are "getting there."

I have no idea what stage of grief you are in. I don't even fully understand what stage(s) I am in. At times, I feel as though I am moving ahead and progressing to the next stage, but then in one short moment, I feel as though I am back at square one again. Sometimes I feel that I am bouncing back and forth between stages more than I should be.

Your emotions resulting from losing different people may be intermingled, as I feel mine are. Resolving these mixed feelings can get rather confusing and complicated. When I stop to consider that I am dealing with multiple losses, I try to give myself some slack.

You may feel that someone who has lost a loved one – maybe the same loved one as you – is not expressing their grief in the "right way." Maybe they don't appear to be as sad as you think they should be. While we should not judge ourselves for how we express our grief, we also must make an effort not to judge others for how they do or do not grieve.

Remember that everyone grieves differently. There is no right or wrong way to go through the process. We should try to not to be critical of others, nor ourselves, for how we grieve and heal.

Chapter 3
The Loss of a Child

If you have lost a spouse and/or a child this year, the Holidays may be extra hard for you. From my perspective, losing a child or my spouse would be the two hardest deaths that I would ever have to face.

Throughout my life, I have been told that God has a plan and a purpose for everything, but the death of a child is something that most of us have a harder time coming to grips with. I have noticed something, though.

I have noticed that parents who seem to have come to terms (as much as possible), with the loss of a child, are those who have tried to create some kind of meaning from the death of their child.

These are the parents who are determined to make sure that their child will not have died "for no reason." They make the choice to take action and try to prevent other parents from losing their children. They may work to get certain laws enacted. They may decide to speak publicly about what could have been done differently. They may write books to help other grieving parents. They do whatever they need to, in the best way they can, to create something positive from their loss.

I have also heard of people who allow these causes to take over their entire lives, thereby neglecting loves ones who are still with them. That's a topic I won't go into here, but it's something to watch for.

If you choose to become active in a cause to honor your loved one this holiday season, start small. You could visit children in a hospital, donate money to an orphanage, or buy toys for the children of families who cannot afford them.

No action you take can fix everything for you, but taking some kind of action in the name of your child may help you through the season. What you choose to do and how you decide to go about it will be a very individual choice.

Please visit www.livingwithoutsomeoneyoulove.com and let us know if you have other suggestions or comments for parents who have lost a child, other than the ones I have mentioned.

Chapter 4
Plan For and Accept Changes

Without your loved one in the picture, the holidays will always feel different to you. Some years you may struggle more and some years you may be fine. However, it will never be quite the same again. (Depending upon your situation, the Holidays might be better than they were in the past, which may mean that your relationship with the deceased person was not a good one. This is another area I won't be addressing in this book).

In both a mental and a physical sense, it is fruitless to try and duplicate past holiday celebrations, like it was before someone's death. The good news is there are some things you can do to prepare yourself and your family for the changes.

Taking some time to plan ahead gives you the opportunity to think about things more calmly, rather than making decisions in the "heat of the moment."

For instance, if your loved one was normally the one who made a certain food and you feel that it would be nice to have that food there, either make it yourself or ask someone else to make it. My mother-in-law had numerous family desert favorites. Over the years, my daughter has been stepping in to help her make some of these deserts. No one in the family has a problem asking my daughter to make any of the deserts her grandmother usually made. For us, it is comforting to have some of these same foods.

If the person who passed away normally did the decorating, ask someone if they would like to handle that this Christmas. If you usually take care of most of the festivity details and you do not feel up to it this year, ask specific people to take over specific jobs. On the other hand, if you feel that some of the normal decorations, food or activities would be too painful this year, you may want to skip them entirely.

Make sure that everyone involved knows what decisions are being made ahead of time and try to give everyone a voice in the decisions that are made.

If your loved one had a particular chair at the table where they sat every year, discuss different seating arrangements in advance. Consider inviting someone who doesn't normally celebrate with you to sit in that place. I know that I would not do it this way, but you may even choose to keep the chair empty in honor of your loved one. Personally, I would not want to see an empty chair at the table with us.

The holidays will come whether you think you are ready for them or not. You may as well be proactive and save you and your family from some painful and uncomfortable moments by planning ahead as much as you can.

Chapter 5
Accept Your Feelings

Expressing your feelings after a loved one's death may feel like a "double-edge sword." On one hand, you don't want to bring anyone down by showing your sadness. On the other hand, if you feel any degree of happiness or find yourself laughing, you may feel guilty.

You don't have to feel badly about not being in constant torment. You are not being disrespectful of your loved one or not honoring them by acting "normal." If you feel like laughing, give into that feeling before it disappears. We need to release some tension now and then during the hard process of grieving.

If you feel like you need to cry your eyes out, do that too. If you have ever had a good cry – and most of us probably have – it can be exhausting, but it can also release pent up emotion that needs to come out.

Your feelings and emotions may run the gamut from anger, sadness and guilt to fear, anxiety and crying. You may feel at peace one moment and in the very next moment feel very sad. Allow yourself to experience your emotions, whatever they may be and whenever they come. (I am not suggesting that if you feel like screaming and venting at someone to go ahead and do that, although there may be a time and a place for that too, depending upon the situation).

If someone asks you how you are doing, don't feel as though you need to say "good" or "just fine." You can tell that person if you're not doing so great or that you're having a bad day or a bad week. You don't have to deny your feelings to yourself or to anyone else.

Often times, people "deal" with their emotions by keeping extremely busy, both physically and mentally. Staying busy can be a good distraction to a certain extent. Giving yourself a break from the grief now and then is very necessary.

However, if you find yourself going at break neck speed day in and day out, it becomes an avoidance issue. If you do not deal with your grief, you may very well be prolonging the process. The way to work through our grief is to do exactly that – you need to grieve.

I know this because I have been spending about 15 hours a day on the computer for most of this year. I have been trying to keep my mind busy so that I do not have to think about the things that make me sad.

That tactic does not work. The first time I lifted my head from the computer to stop and think about things, everything hit me at once. I started crying and literally could not stop for several weeks. Because I had not been processing the deaths in my family as they happened, I ended up dealing with them all at once.

There were other things going on during this time frame that added to the stress. My job was cut, my husband and I became empty-nesters and I have been going through menopause (sorry guys).

You too will have other issues that come up, which may add to your level of anxiety. Between these "other" things, the death of a loved one, and the holiday season, you many have a lot to deal with. Don't suppress your emotions. Accept and process your feelings as they come, rather than having everything hit you at the same time. It will be easier to deal with them bit-by-bit.

While you need to address your emotions, I would suggest that you not go chasing after them either. Especially at first, you may want to avoid things that you know are going to make you sad. Today is the day before Thanksgiving in the United States and I have already been hearing Christmas songs on the radio for the past several days. Some years it is just too hard to listen to songs like "I'll be home for Christmas" and "Blue Christmas." Don't listen to seasonal songs if they bring you down. Turn the radio station or put on a CD that you know won't have any Christmas music on it.

Besides varying emotions, you may also experience physical symptoms caused by grief, ranging from stomach aches, fatigue and headaches to having trouble breathing and chest pain. You may have "panic attacks," which www.mayoclinic.org describes as "a sudden episode of intense fear that triggers severe physical reactions when there is no real danger or apparent cause."

Panic attacks can be very frightening. When panic attacks occur, you might think you're losing control, having a heart attack or even dying. Panic attacks can have numerous and varied symptoms. I have had three panic attacks that I can remember in my life time. I don't remember that any of them were related to someone's death.

The reason that I even mention panic attacks is so that you are aware of them and know that you cannot die from having one. To lessen the chance of getting a panic attack, learn about how to prevent them. The Mayo Clinic web site, as well as numerous other sites, offer lots of helpful information on this topic.

Since your emotions may be very volatile this time of year and you may not be your "normal" self, be careful with the kinds of decisions that you make, especially if they are bigger decisions. Put off certain decisions until you are better equipped to handle them.

For instance, don't throw out all the Christmas decorations. Don't sell your home or move out of town. Don't give away all your loved one's possessions. Don't do these things when your emotions are at their rawest, which may include the holiday season. Make decisions when your head is clear, so that you don't find yourself regretting a hasty decision later on.

During the grieving process, how you feel about specific things or issues may also vary. Let me give you an example.

My mother-in-law (Pat) and I wore the same size clothes. After she passed away, the other women in the family said that I should keep some of Pat's clothes. At first, I was hesitant to take any of these items, but I did pick out some clothes and put them in my car, where they stayed for quite some time.

Eventually, I put the clothes in my closet. When I first started wearing some of Pat's things, it felt odd. I could still smell her scent in the clothes, even after they were washed. I almost felt as though I had stolen them.

Pat's scent is gradually fading out of her clothes every time I wear them and with every wash. However, now I find myself sniffing her blouses and sweatshirts because the scent has become comforting to me. I am glad that I took some of the clothes she used to wear. If I had not taken them, when I was more emotional about her death, I would have missed out on having these comforting physical reminders with me.

You can always change your mind, but it is better to keep things for now and decide later what you would like to do with them.

CHAPTER 6
LOOK TO GOD

Talk to God (or whoever you pray to if you do pray) and ask him to give you strength for each day. I know people who have lost loved ones and felt that they would never be happy again. They prayed to God and trusted that they would be taken care of and they were. You would never recognize that they were the same people based on their outlook today.

I believe that we have a wonderful God who will welcome us into heaven. I can visualize my loved ones dancing and doing all of the things that they were no longer able to do on earth. I am looking forward to dancing with them again one day. Sometimes, I almost envy them.

At Christmas time, I am renewed in my faith. I wish this for you too, especially this year. I ask you to open your mind and heart to what God can do for you and give him the chance.

Chapter 7
Take Care of Yourself Physically and Emotionally

We all know that in order to stay healthy, there are certain things we need to do and certain things we need to avoid.

Eating a healthy, balanced diet is critical to our health. Yet, based on the growing number of obese people in the world, it's very obvious many of us do not make the right choices, even when we know what is and is not good for us.

People going through the grieving process are more susceptible to illness because their system is experiencing so many changes and stressors. This is why it is even more important at this time to take care of your body.

During the holiday season, unhealthy foods and drinks seem to be everywhere. It seems as though there is a contest as to who can bring the dish with the highest fat content and the most sugar – otherwise known as comfort foods!

If you are asked what kind of food you would like brought to your house for a gathering, do not be afraid to be specific. Request healthier foods - those that do not contain so many starches, fats and sugar – be brought to your home. You could even ask people to cut up some fresh fruit and vegetables for you. When you feel as though you have no energy or desire to do much of anything, little things like this can really increase your chances of eating healthier.

With three family members passing away in less than a three-month period, I ate an abundance of what I call "funeral food." My family and I put away more deep fried foods, desserts and starches during that time frame than we probably had eaten within the last five years.

Don't rely on junk food because it's quicker and easier to prepare. You may get a temporary "high" from eating these kinds of foods, but the slump that you will feel later is not worth it.

During the holidays, there also seems to be an abundance of alcoholic beverages wherever you go. A glass of wine or a serving of beer is not going to be your end-all.

However, because of your emotional state, you may be less resistant to alcohol than you normally are. Alcohol might affect you more because of your current emotional state. Once you start using alcohol to make you feel better, you may find yourself relying on it more than you intended to. At that point, it is usually much harder to cut back or give it up.

For me personally, alcohol, especially wine, usually makes me very moody and tired. If you are like me, your best bet is to avoid alcohol all together and stick with non-alcoholic drinks, especially water. Drinking plenty of water can drastically improve your energy level, as well as your physical and emotional well-being. If you feel lethargic or sense a headache coming on, a cure might be as easy as a tall glass of water!

Try to get some exercise every day, even if it is in short chunks. It may be very hard to motivate yourself to get going, but getting started is usually the hardest part.

If you keep at it on a regular basis, you will have more energy over-all. Exercising also reduces stress. When I am on a treadmill or swimming and going hard at it, I am so focused on my workout, that there is no energy left over for negative thoughts. Physically and mentally, I am getting a much needed break from whatever is stressing me out. If you are not currently exercising, remember to start out in small increments, so that you don't end up with sore muscles.

Get enough fresh air and vitamin D. Exercise outside if you can. If you exercise inside, get at least 20 minutes of sunshine on a daily basis when possible. If you live in Minnesota like I do, chances are you cannot be outside very long for many months of the year because it is just too frigid. I try to get outside every day because our dog needs to get the exercise. However, I am so bundled up that virtually the only areas of my skin which have a chance of getting any sunlight are my nose and lips.

Those of us who live in a northern climate often suffer from SAD – seasonal affective disorder.

Because we get so little sunlight, we may fall into a depressive state. This is a real and common disorder. You should be aware of it, because if you are already suffering mentally and/or physically due to grieving, your symptoms may very well be compounded by SAD if you are not getting enough sunshine.

I do two things during the long winter months to help me from feeling these winter blues. I take a vitamin D supplement and I use light therapy.

You are fairly safe taking a vitamin D supplement, but if it makes you feel more comfortable, have a doctor check your vitamin D level to see how much you need. If you don't feel like you are being taken seriously by your medical doctor, consult a homeopathic doctor for guidance in this area. I notice a big drop in my energy level when I do not take a vitamin D supplement in the winter months.

Light therapy involves using special lamps to simulate sunlight. The light sends a message to the part of our brain that resets our inner body clock. Light therapy can stimulate sleep, relaxation and hormone production.

I use a sun lamp for several hours each day. The best time to use light therapy is in the morning. Avoid using the lamp in the evening because it may end up keeping you awake instead of helping you get your sleep!

On the subject of sleep and proper rest, put a priority on that, versus making sure your house is in perfect order or doing the last bit of ironing. Catch up on your rest with an afternoon nap when you need to.

(Regarding the condition of your home, ask for help if you need help cleaning it. Having physical chaos in your life, especially when you are not used to it, can contribute to emotional chaos).

Hopefully, you are not relying on any kind of non-prescribed drugs as a cure for grieving. This includes the use of sleeping aids. Your doctor may prescribe sleeping pills if you are having issues with getting enough sleep, but if abused or used for too long, sleeping aids can cause their own set of problems.

I have used sleeping pills off and on at different points in my life. I have found several disadvantages to relying on them on a regular basis.

The first disadvantage of taking sleep medications is that their effect seems to wear off after you have taken them for a while. Then, when you need them most, they don't work for you. A second drawback is that you become so dependent on them you cannot sleep without them. Another problem with sleeping medications is that even though you may sleep more hours at night, you may wake up feeling groggy the next day. It may end up being a "trade-off."

If you are tempted to use drugs and/or alcohol to make yourself feel better, distract yourself instead with healthier options. Listen to pleasant music, take a warm and soothing bath or visit with someone who cares about you.

There is a reason they call drugs, drinking and over-eating "quick fixes." It's because they never work in the long run. They may temporarily help you put your grieving on the back burner, but the only thing which will really help you is to face your situation and find healthier ways to heal.

Chapter 8
Make Time for Yourself

You need some time alone to process both your loss and the changes it will bring to your life. You can use this time to renew yourself. You can also use the time to vent, scream and cry if you need to. If you are someone who does not want to make public displays of emotion, releasing some of your strongest feelings in private will make it easier to maintain your composure in public.

You could use the time alone to write in a journal. Many people work through a lot of emotion and are able to process their thoughts and feelings by putting them in writing. Write to the person you are now missing. Express yourself freely when you are writing. There will be no one judging you on what you say, think or feel.

It is emotionally exhausting to have company all of the time. As comforting as it may be to have people around after someone passes away, you need a break now and then. Do not be afraid to tell people you need to be alone for a while.

However, there is a difference between being alone and being lonely.

It is not healthy if you are alone and feel like hurting yourself. It is not healthy to be alone for days at a time. It is not healthy to be alone and dwelling on how badly you feel. Do not wait to talk to someone if you are by yourself and feel yourself sinking deeper and deeper into despair.

Decide to act right then and there to contact someone who you can spend time with. Do not wait until you feel so badly or are so lonely that you don't have the energy or the desire to take action to help yourself.

If you are thinking about hurting yourself and do not want to call anyone that you know, the **National Suicide Hotline number is: 800-273-8255.**

Most people do not reach the point where they need to call a suicide prevention number, but this is one case where it is always better to be safe than sorry.

Chapter 9
Ask for Support and Help

While you do need time alone, you also need to be around people who love and support you. Having support after someone's death can be a life saver. Social support and distraction can be very healing and being alone during the holidays can be especially lonely and painful.

You do not want to isolate yourself from others who can help you through this process, especially if they are suffering from the same loss. Sharing a loss can be very comforting.

Sometimes, when you allow others to help, you may actually be helping *them* out at the same time.

When I found out that my brother, Bruce was very ill and that he would not live much longer, there was not much that I could do for him and his family because we lived a few states apart. I decided to do something that would help Bruce's two children remember their Dad. I rounded up all the pictures I could find of Bruce, beginning with his hospital baby picture. I made copies of the pictures and created two identical scrapbooks, which told the story of his life in pictures. I put many hours into those two books.

While it was definitely a labor of love, it was also very healing for me to create those albums. Putting them together brought back many fond memories of growing up with Bruce and it temporarily softened the blow of the reality for me. I finished the albums a few days before Bruce passed away and he was able to see them. They were then given to his children.

Making those scrap books was probably a bigger gift to myself than it was for Bruce and his family. You may very well be doing someone a favor when you allow them to do something for you.

When people offer to help you, take them up on their offer and do not be afraid to ask for help, even if it is not offered. People often don't know how they can help you best. Be specific about what you need and do not be afraid to make suggestions.

If you need help cleaning your house or cooking meals, ask someone to help with those things. If you need someone to just listen to you or to be with you, tell them that too.

Being specific with what you need will benefit both you and others who want to help you out.

Chapter 10
Be Realistic With Expectations of Yourself

The holidays are filled with so many expectations. These expectations include how we are supposed to feel this time of year, which is happy and excited, of course. Expectations also include what we are supposed to accomplish, such as buying Christmas gifts, serving wonderful meals and having our house look perfect.

Some of these expectations are "put upon" us by others, while some we impose upon ourselves. All of these expectations can really wear us down. We need to give ourselves a break, especially if we have lost someone this past year. (Women especially, seem to put a lot of unnecessary pressure on themselves).

Make this year different. Decide that you do not have to do everything you have done in past holidays.

Look at the things that are most important to you and your family, and if you feel that you can accomplish these things, then go ahead and do them.

Do not feel as though you need to attend every holiday gathering you are invited to – or any of them if you don't want to. If you do attend an event, people who care about you should understand if you are not upbeat the entire time. If you feel like going for just a short time, maybe give it a go.

Emotions from our grief can be unpredictable and hit us when we least expect it. You might accept an invitation to a gathering one day, and when that day comes, you may not feel up to attending the event after all. When you are invited to a gathering during the holidays, tell people you will plan on attending, but not to count on you 100%. Then, if you don't feel up to it when the day of the event comes, you've given yourself an out. Only attend the events you think you might enjoy.

If you normally host or entertain for the holidays, ask for help or ask someone else to completely take it over. You do not need to exert the energy to entertain, unless it is truly something you enjoy doing.

For many years, my husband and I would fight every Christmas Eve because I had such high expectations of how I wanted things to be. When I could not accomplish everything I wanted to, I would get frustrated because he would not pitch in to help me. Part of my frustration also hinged on the fact that he waited until Christmas Eve to shop for presents. On Christmas morning, he was in the kitchen finishing up cookies and baking pies. Meanwhile, I was getting three young children ready to go out of town and finishing up the packing. It was never the idyllic Christmas morning I was hoping for.

After losing both of my parents, as well as his parents, my husband and I have learned to cut each other some slack. Looking back in time, my ideas of what I thought "had to be done" were actually quite silly. I still don't care for my husband's last minute shopping tactics and waiting until Christmas day to do his baking.

However, I have since learned to appreciate the fact that he even does that baking, which I do not like to do. I have also quit putting so much stock into trivial things, such as how the house looks.

I used to send out Christmas cards every single year. About 15 years ago, I began sending them out every other year and about five years ago, I started sending them out any time after the second of January.

I finally decided that it really did not matter what time of year I let people know I was thinking about them. People get so many cards all at once in December; maybe they appreciate getting a card or two separate from the influx of the others that hit their mail boxes at the same time of year.

Do not worry about sending Christmas cards out at all if you do not feel up to it. The year my Mom passed away a few days before Thanksgiving was especially hard, so I am sure that was one year I did not send cards out. (I still make sure that we take our annual Christmas picture; I just don't go through the effort of mailing the pictures).

We stress ourselves out doing so many unnecessary things, especial during the holidays. The ironic part is (sorry to burst your bubble), most people probably don't even notice if you don't send them a card every year.

You may want to only send cards this year to people who might not be aware of the death of your loved one. You will probably be doing them a favor. They would probably want to know about the death and would appreciate the opportunity to express their condolences.

If you still want to buy gifts this year, consider toning it down. Purchase gift cards this year. Shop by phone, the internet, or mail order catalogs. Maybe you need to completely rid yourself of the pressure of buying gifts this year. (In this instance, I am referring to other adults that you usually give gifts to. Never skip buying gifts for the children in your life!)

Happy events, such as a baptism, can be stressful too. No matter what the event, it will take time and energy from you. When you are deciding whether or not to accept an invitation, take this into account when you are filling in dates on your calendar.

Many people completely wear themselves out during the holidays. You may already have your hands full just dealing with your loss. Don't push yourself so hard. At least for this year, do yourself a favor and slow down a bit.

Chapter 11
Talk about Your Loved One

Sometimes people don't know what to say to someone who is grieving. Or, they may feel that talking about the person who is gone is will upset you or make you sad. Sometimes people don't say anything because they themselves are unable to talk about the death. So they say nothing at all. It can cause hurt feelings and get very uncomfortable. The topic is like an elephant in the room.

It may be left up to you to bring up the name of your loved one. Let others know that you need to talk about this person and that you also want them to feel free to talk about her or him.

During the holidays, when you are all together, encourage others to share good memories and stories about the person who passed away. Ask everyone to write down a fond memory of that person and share what they wrote. Together, look at photos of that person.

Sharing your sadness with those who were close to the same person may help lighten your load.

If you say grace before meals, include the deceased in your prayers. One of my brothers, Tim, who is a priest, is very good about including all of those who have passed away in the prayers we say before our holiday meals. I think I can speak for everyone in my family when I say we appreciate and are glad Tim includes those who are no longer with us when we are giving thanks to God.

Talking about our loved ones may make us a little teary-eyed or worse, but we need to do so because it really does help.

Chapter 12
Honor Your Loved One

Besides talking about our loved one, we can also include them in the holidays in many different ways. The following are some examples of how we can do this.

- Take holiday decorations to the cemetery.
- Have a moment of silence each time you get together during the holidays to honor your loved one.
- Dedicate one of the Chanukah candles in memory of your loved one.
- Play your loved one's favorite music or play a game that he/she enjoyed.
- Hang a Christmas stocking with your loved one's name on it.
- Light a candle in his/her honor.
- Buy a special ornament in their memory.
- Cook that person's favorite food.
- Create a memory box filled with special mementos.
- Have a mass said in honor of that person.

You can honor the life of your loved one throughout your life in many different ways. Paying a special tribute during the holidays, surrounded by others who also loved that person, makes it even more meaningful.

Chapter 13
Blend Old and New Traditions

One of the hardest parts of the holidays can be dealing with traditions after a death in the family. The same rituals that used to bring you so much joy can now be painful.

There are basically three different ways you can deal with family traditions.

The first choice is to try and do everything exactly the same way you have always done it. This can be very difficult both physically and emotionally, depending upon what roles your loved ones played in your traditions. You won't be able to re-create things exactly as they have always been and the more you try, the more noticeable that person's absence may be.

Another possibility is to do everything completely different.

This can be hard too because you will probably find yourself really missing some of the normal activities and traditions.

The third choice is to combine old traditions along with creating new traditions. This option can give you the opportunity to keep important connections with the person who died, yet still give you and your family a sense of moving forward.

On my husband's side of the family, our Christmas celebrations will be very different this year. Since both of my husband's parents died this past year and their house has been sold, we will no longer have these two family patriarchs to celebrate the holidays with.

The physical venue, as well as all the traditional decorating and almost all of the food will be different. We have been celebrating Christmas the same way, with the same people, at the same location for 29 years. Our children have never known anything different. Several months ago we decided who would be hosting Thanksgiving Day and Christmas Day. For adults and children alike, knowing what to expect helps ease some of the fears and uncertainties.

We have no control over when our loved ones pass away, but this does not mean we cannot choose to take control of how we celebrate the holidays in the future. Having a sense of control is helpful to us emotionally.

By the time the Thanksgiving holiday arrived this year, I had painted my living room walls and had new flooring installed in my living room and hallway. I am hoping these physical changes in our daily surroundings, which have been the same for almost 20 years, will psychologically help my family prepare for this Christmas.

I am saying "Yes, you can expect that not everything will look and feel the same this holiday season, but things will still be okay." It's what I consider a proactive and healthy way of gaining some control over the situation. In a sense, I am trying to "pull us forward."

After you decide what traditions you want to keep, you and your family can come up with some ideas for trying some new things.

Some of the options can include the following:

- Have your holiday meals at a different house.
- Change the menu a bit.
- Eat out at a restaurant versus eating at someone' home. (You also won't have to worry about cleaning up afterwards).
- Open gifts at a different location than you normally do.
- If you attend religious services, go to a different place of worship or worship at a different time of day.
- Take a trip over the holidays. This means that the next year may feel like your first "real holiday" without your loved ones and after the passage of time, you may be better prepared emotionally.

If something you try this year doesn't feel quite right, you can always try something different next year. Nothing needs to be written in stone. Just go with what feels right.

Chapter 14
Focus on the Children

Children make everything more special, and that certainly includes the holidays.

Children give you the opportunity to literally "stop and smell the roses." They are focused on the moment at hand and are able to enjoy what is right in front of them. Kids can teach us a lot about how we should spend our time and direct our energy.

In 1997 my town and the neighboring town were turned upside down by a "100-year flood." Almost everyone in the two towns lost their homes – either temporarily or permanently. My family and I were in the "middle," and returned to our home after about ten months.

When the flood hit, I had been running a home-daycare business, which meant our family not only lost that income, but the kid's daily lifestyle was uprooted overnight. For many months, when my husband came home from his job, he would work on getting the basic structure of the house back together.

Meanwhile, my job was to take care of the "other" things. Some of these other things included lining up the flooring for the house, ordering kitchen cupboards, locating furniture, painting the walls, staining the woodwork and numerous other jobs. I also needed to put my home daycare business back together.

That was the easy part. What made it so challenging was that I had all three children with me 24 hours a day. At the time, they were 20 months, four years and seven years old. You can probably imagine what it was like trying to accomplish some of these things with three small children!

I remember one trip to the carpet store in particular. The kids were excited to get out, so they were all over the place, crawling on top of, inside and behind the rolls of carpet. It was exhausting trying to make choices about flooring, while talking to salespeople and constantly stopping to chase after the kids to keep them within my view. I had a lot of moments and days like that.

But even then, I knew I was very fortunate. Those three children of mine, while physically exhausting me, were my personal saviors. Because I needed to focus on the needs of my kids, I really did not have much time or energy to dwell on the situation we were in. (I do give myself credit as a mother, though, because I worked hard that spring, summer and fall to create fun and enjoyment for the kids whenever I could).

Because of my children, I was able to focus on small treasures now and then, such as watching a ladybug crawl in the park, smelling a pretty flower or having a picnic in the park. Doing those things made it easier to look at the immediate picture, which took my mind off bigger worries.

Admittedly, it was hard for me to slow down and make the time to do some of those things with the kids, but I am so thankful we did.

During those months after the flood, we lived in several temporary locations, with our whole family often not being together for days or weeks at a time. As an adult, those times were unsettling to me, so I can only imagine how upsetting everything was for my children.

Although my family and I did not lose anyone to the flood, we did suffer other losses. Those other losses included all of our possessions, one –half of our income, our home, and any kind of normalcy in our lives for over a year.

Just as my children expressed their grieving in various ways after the flood, you too should be prepared that the children in your life will have different ways of expressing their grief after someone's death.

When adults grieve, it is usually quite obvious. However, children seem to have a different way of grieving. Children may do things such as acting out, have separation anxiety, and regress back to certain stages, such as thumb-sucking or bed-wetting, crying and temper tantrums.

My brother and my brother-in-law both died quite early in their lives– both just after they had turned 40. When these two dads died, they left behind a total of five children, ranging in ages from three to fourteen. All of these children were very close to their fathers. I remember thinking how well they seemed to be handling things – almost "too well."

While children do often grieve differently than adults, it does not mean they grieve any less. They can only express their grief based upon their personal capabilities and their physical age.

I remember hearing a psychologist say that with adults, the impact from a death often hits harder and faster, and then progressively gets better. When a child loses someone, the impact is more sporadic. There may be more moments during their lifetime where the loss will hit them "out-of-the-blue," especially during events like graduation, weddings and the birth of their own children.

Children may have to learn how to cope all over again - many times in their lives - as they move from childhood into adulthood.

Even if children do not seem to have a need to talk about the death, it is very important to give them ample time and opportunity to do so. If they are at an age where they cannot express themselves well, or they simply cannot bring themselves to talk about it, spending extra time with them will help you both with healing. They need to know that you are still there for them.

It's okay to show your emotions around children. They need to be reassured that they can express their feelings in healthy ways. However, it's not healthy for anyone if the kids see you continuously withdrawing from everyone and appear to be sad most of the time.

Of the traditions and physical reminders that you do decide to keep, hold on to the things that are most important to the children. It will help keep some stability in their lives.

When bad things happen that we cannot control, we feel so powerless. The situation is usually worse for children because they have even less of a voice than adults do concerning decisions to be made.

Remember to include children in the decision-making when possible. Allow them to give their opinions about how things should be done this holiday season.

During the holidays, especially when the pace of life picks up and emotions may be running high from both a death in the family and the holidays, be prepared that your children may "act up" a bit more than they usually do. Your best bet is to try to keep things as normal as possible and make sure that everyone, including you, gets enough rest.

Slow down as often as possible to cherish and appreciate the children in your life. It will make the tough times easier for all concerned.

Chapter 15
Be Thankful

Sometimes it takes someone's death to realize how lucky we are, especially when we take into account the people that we still have in our lives. The death of someone can help us see the "big picture" and open our eyes as to how we should be spending the rest of our time on earth.

I am not suggesting that the "trade-off" is worth it, but you could try and view this insight as a gift from your loved one.

Let me give you an example. My neighbor and I, who used to be quite close, quit talking to each other for several years. What put a rift between us was her dog, which seemed to bark 24 hours a day. It drove me crazy and when I finally told her so, she did nothing to change the situation.

Our being at odds with each other probably bothered her as much as it bothered me. I wanted to mend the fences, but I didn't know how to go about it and I was a little afraid of having my attempt at reconciliation rejected. (That was my excuse, anyway). It was not until the death of my mother-in-law that the fences were mended.

One day, my neighbor dropped by bringing a condolence card and telling us that she was sorry for our loss. That was all it took to get us talking again and since then, things have been (practically) normal between the two of us. We are not only on speaking terms again, but we are even doing things small favors for each other again.

This Christmas will be the first time in over five years that I will be sending her a Christmas card. I have to smile when I think how tickled my mother-in-law would be to know this. She was even a blessing to me after her death.

Maybe your loved one's death will change you in a positive way. You may find yourself being kinder to others, mending fences, and putting a higher priority on your relationships with people.

Celebrate your loved one's life by living your best life and by not taking anyone for granted. We need to grieve, but we can still be thankful at the same time. We can use the grief to help us see all the good things that exist in our lives.

The degree of pain we feel today from not having that person physically with us any longer, is the degree of thankfulness we should feel for having had that person in our life in the first place.

Chapter 16
Do Something for Someone Else

Probably one of the last things on your mind right now is reaching out to help others. After all, you are struggling with having lost a loved one and the holidays are already keeping you busy. You may wonder how you could possibly find the time, energy or desire to help anyone else right now.

Did you know that the act of doing for others can actually help you heal from your loss? There are many benefits that you will reap from giving.

People who give to others are usually more satisfied with their own life than those who don't give.

Givers are more able to cope with difficulties in their lives than non-givers and givers are generally healthier and don't suffer from anxiety and depression as much as those who do not give. Helping others gives meaning to your life and gives your life more purpose.

In fact, the "giver" usually benefits more from the act of giving than the one on the receiving end. The reason for this is because it isn't possible to feel negative emotions when we are involved in kind and compassionate acts. While you are thinking about another person, you aren't dwelling on your own problems. Your stress levels drop. You may also realize how much you have, especially in comparison to those to whom you are giving.

Either financially or physically – or maybe both – there are many options for helping someone else. The following are some things that you can do during the holiday season:

- Help a cause your loved one either supported or one you think he or she may have been interested in supporting.
- Use the money you would have spent for a gift for your loved one to buy something for someone else.

- Find a family in the area who could use your financial help.
- Visit with someone who lives alone or someone you think may be lonely. People in retirement homes are always happy to have someone visit them, even if they don't personally know you.
- Take meals to people who cannot leave their homes.
- Volunteer at a shelter.
- Ring the bell for the Salvation Army.

Remember that you are not only helping those to whom you give, but you are also helping yourself along the road to recovery.

Chapter 17
Look Forward with a Positive Attitude

We all have more control than we realize over how we feel and what happens to us. Trying to stay positive, even in the worst of times, such as after someone's death, can help get us back on the path to normalcy.

You are facing a big setback, but with perseverance, you will recover. Try to be strong and look at life's problems as challenges. Remind yourself that you are a capable person and you can face your challenges with action instead of fear and self-pity.

Your positive thoughts can actually help create positive outcomes. By repeating positive affirmations, you will become a positive person. Visualize a good future for yourself.

Work towards happiness. Do your best to create a happy environment for yourself. When you are feeling down, take some action to uplift your spirit. Spend time with children, watch a funny movie, or visit with an up-beat friend.

What has happened is irreversible and we do not know what the future will bring, so try to find some enjoyment in each day. Set short-term, mid-range and long-term goals for yourself at different intervals on the calendar. This will give you something to look forward to and reasons to get up each day.

As an example, I am looking forward to spending time with my sister and her husband tomorrow. In about a month, my son will be home for college for a few weeks and a few months after that, my husband and I will be taking a trip to someplace warmer. A few years down the road I hope to have grandchildren.

When you are ready to, consider going back to school; it will give you goals to shoot for and keep you mentally alert. If you live alone, pets make wonderful companions; they are non-judgmental and very good listeners.

If you have not been working, think about getting a part-time job; you will not only have some extra income, but probably meet some new people.

Positive changes will not happen overnight, but a firm commitment to do your best is a good start.

Chapter 18
If You Know Someone Who Is Grieving

Turn the coin over for a minute. Perhaps you are not the one who is grieving at this time. Maybe you know someone who has lost a loved one this past year and you are wondering how you can help them.

Think about what you appreciated others doing for you when you lost a loved one. If you have never lost someone close to you, stop and think for a moment how that might feel and what you might need from others. Whatever ideas came into your head just now are probably the same things someone else would benefit from.

The following are suggestions for what you can do for someone who is grieving this holiday season:

- Support that person with however they decide to handle the holidays.

- Offer to help with baking and/or cleaning. You may remember how exhausting those chores were for you when you were experiencing your worst times.

- Offer to help decorate their home for the holidays.
- Ask them if they would like help with holiday shopping.
- If you attend religious services, invite them to go with you.
- Invite them to your home for the holidays.
- Help them with their holiday cards.
- Invite them to do some volunteering with you.
- Donate a gift or money in memory of that person's loved one and tell them you did so.

There are things that you can do year-round for someone who is grieving. Be a good listener when the person who is grieving wants to talk about the person they lost or about how they feel. You don't need to come up with the "right" answers or try to "solve" their grief. That is something that they will need to work out on their own. Allow them to cry when they need to.

Don't be afraid to talk about the person who passed away. Grieving people want to know that their loved one has not been forgotten.

Grieving people usually do not want to hear trite sayings such as "he/she is in a better place, "or "at least they are not suffering anymore" or "God needed her/him in heaven."
Even if you have suffered a loss yourself, try not to say "I know how you feel," because you don't. Everyone has their own unique thoughts, feelings and connections with their loved one.

People may be unsure about what to do or say after someone dies, so they might not do or say anything. After someone loses a loved one, it is important that you acknowledge the loss. A simple "I am sorry for your loss," may be all you need to say.

Not addressing the death can cause hurt and resentment. It may inadvertently send the message that you do not care enough about either the person who died - or the person suffering the loss - to make the effort to acknowledge the death.

This may sound harsh, but I have been that person many times to whom nothing was said after someone I love died.

Until you have lost someone close to you, you may not realize how important it is to acknowledge someone's loss. I will tell you now that it is very important.

Even if you feel a bit uncomfortable or awkward saying something, you need to express your condolences - in both actions and words

One of the most important things that you can do for someone who is grieving is to simply be there for them. When someone dies, there is usually an abundance of people around at first, but then that number soon dwindles down to nothing, or close to it.

Your life may go on as normal, but those who were close to the deceased person do not get to experience that for what may be a very long time. Be consistent and continue to visit, call, or write. Stay in touch.

Chapter 19
More Resources and Support

I hope you have friends and family helping you get through this tough time. If you do not, there are resources which exist to help you. Even if you do have plenty of family and friends, you may feel they have no idea what you are going through. You may want to talk to others who can relate to your current situation better.

Check out what kind of support groups exist where you live. Sharing with others can lighten your load, especially when they are also grieving the loss of someone.

Hospice was a wonderful resource we used when both my Mom and my brother were dying from cancer. Hospice is a program for terminally ill patients and their families. All hospices offer certain services, which usually, if not always includes help with bereavement after your loved one has passed away.

The National Association for Home Care and Hospice is at this site: http://www.nahc.org/

The National hospice agency locator can be found at this web site: http://www.nahcagencylocator.com

This Hospice page also has some good information on bereavement: http://hospicenet.org/

Online support groups are also available to you. However, if you are going to go this route, I would get a recommendation for a group from a reliable source, such as a hospital or Hospice before you start sharing information about yourself over the internet.

Check with your church to see what they may have to offer. Resources to help grieving people during the holidays may exist more frequently than at other times of the year.

Read articles and books, such as this one, about healthy ways to grieve. One book that I refer to now and then is called "A Time to Grieve," written by Carol Staudacher. This book has very short chapters, with many different topics about grieving. When you are having an issue with something in particular, you can reference that particular topic. There are also many thought-inspiring and beautiful quotes in this book that may help you through a particular moment or time.

Search the internet and ask people what they do for hobbies and past times. Finding a good, creative outlet to keep your thoughts and hands busy can be a great stress reliever.

If the resources in this book do not seem to be helping you, or if you feel that your healing is taking longer than you think it should, think about seeing a professional counselor, otherwise known as a psychotherapist.

Psychotherapy is the word used for treating mental health problems by talking with a psychiatrist, psychologist or other mental health provider. It may help to talk to someone who has seen many others through the same process that you are now going through. Most insurances are really good about covering these services.

I honestly cannot remember ever reading a self-help book that suggested using prescription medication to help you through this time, but I am going to ask you to be open to the idea. Clinical depression is very real and it can get worse after someone you love passes away, especially during the holidays.

Chances are, if you were not using a prescription medication for anxiety and/or depression before your loved one's death, your doctor may tell you that you can quit taking the prescription when you feel better.

Many people think that feeling low or not being happy is "normal." You may find that staying on a prescription can help you with problems you were dealing with even before your loss.

I have been on an anxiety/depression medication for many years now. I cannot imagine going back to the way I felt for several years before I started taking this medication. I am a much more capable and happy person that I was before I was on the prescription. In fact, I am a much healthier and more adaptable person than most people I know. That is not only good for me, but good for those around me as well. You may have to try one or two different medications before you find one that works well for you. Don't give up right away.

Some people say that medications are for those who are not strong enough to handle their problems. I contend that it is just the opposite. Those who care about themselves and those they love are the strong ones.

Have you given yourself time to heal? Have you tried different alternatives to make your life better, including seeing a therapist?

If you have tried other options to improve your mental health and feel that you are not progressing, do not ever feel ashamed or embarrassed about visiting with a doctor regarding medication.

You are not being weak or lazy. You are being proactive and strong by seeking help for a life which can be better – a life that you deserve.

Often, a combination of prescription medication and professional counseling may be the optimal way to go until you feel better.

Chapter 20
All We Can Do Is Our Best

We cannot change the way things are and bring our loved one(s) back. However, we can make the choice to tackle our grief head on and make up our mind to do the best we can. For now, we just need to take one step at a time and get from one moment to the next. We can take comfort in the fact that it is temporary; we will get back on track and feel better.

You will have moments of emptiness and loss during the holidays and other days after losing someone you love. These same emotions will help you get through this.

Experiencing your emotions will help get you to where you need to be in order to be happy again. There will come a day when you will look forward to the holidays and every other day.

I do not believe those who have gone before us would want either you or I to enjoy the holidays any less without their presence. If I were to pass away tomorrow, I would want my family to continue carrying out the many traditions and happy memories that we created together over the years.

Things will always be different after losing someone, but it does not mean they will always be bad.

You will always miss your loved one but your loss and pain will eventually be replaced by thankfulness and fullness of heart for having known that person.

I am not a professional grief counselor nor do I profess to have all the answers that you may be looking for. However, I am someone who has lost numerous loved ones and I can tell you with certainty - things will get better.

The death of those we love and the grieving we do for them is all part of life and being human. We cannot have one without the other. We would not be experiencing the sorrow and sadness now if we had not also reaped the joy and the blessings.

The big difference is, the sorrow and sadness we feel today will one day ease, but the blessings and joy will remain with us until the end of our own days.

I sincerely express my condolences if you have experienced the loss of a loved one. I hope you are able to use some of the suggestions and resources in this book and that my words have brought you some amount of peace and hope. I wish you a blessed Holiday season this year and every year!

Please feel free to visit:
www.livingwithoutsomeoneyoulove.com and leave a comment with us. Thank you again for giving me the opportunity to reach out to you.

If you know of others who could benefit from this book, please mention it to them. Also, if you have benefited in any way from reading this book yourself, please go to www.amazon.com and leave a review for me!

Sincerely,

Jayne Flaagan

To learn more about the author and for more insight on this topic, visit www.livingwithoutsomeoneyoulove.com.

When you leave your email address on the web site, we will send you our list of "Loving Messages for Sympathy Cards." (You will never have to worry about wondering what to write in a condolence card again!)

We will also let you know when the next free Kindle download will be offered for this book, as well as other future books written by this same author.

www.ingramcontent.com/pod-product-compliance
Lightning Source LLC
Chambersburg PA
CBHW032047290426
44110CB00012B/992